This **Picture Mammoth** *belongs to*

_____

_____

Dedicated to Nigel, Ben and George

First published in Great Britain 1997
by Heinemann Young Books
Published 1998 by Mammoth
an imprint of Reed International Books Ltd
Michelin House, 81 Fulham Road, London SW3 6RB
10 9 8 7 6 5 4 3 2 1

Copyright © Melanie 1997
Melanie Walsh has asserted her moral rights

ISBN 0 7497 3425 6

A CIP catalogue record for this title
is available from the British Library

Printed in Hong Kong by Wing King Tong Co. Ltd.

Do Monkeys Tweet?

Melanie Walsh

Do horses bark?

woof!

woof!

No, dogs do.

woof! woof!

Do little
mice purr?

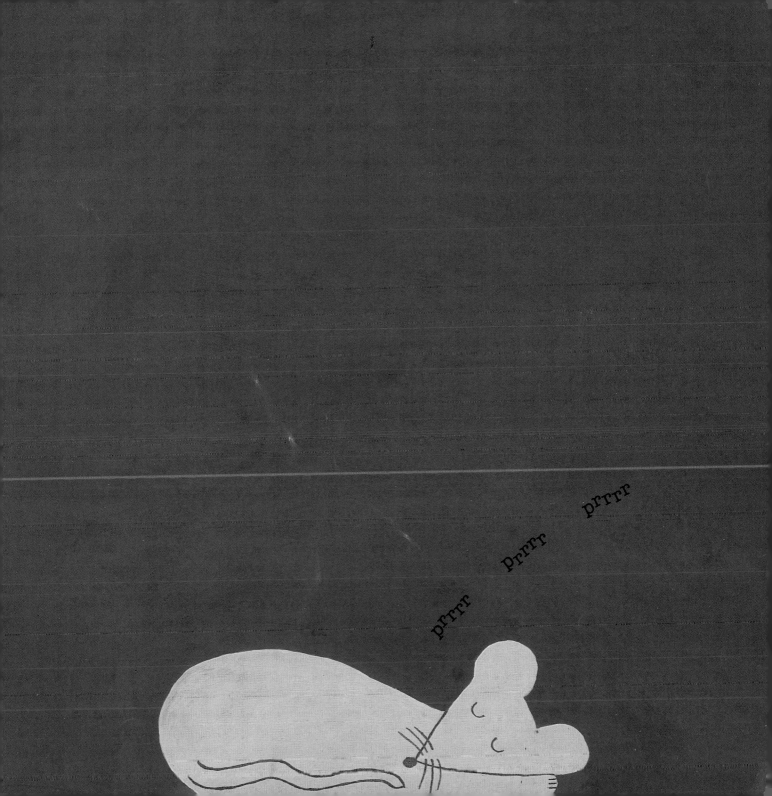

No, pussy cats purr.

Do baby lambs go

buzz?

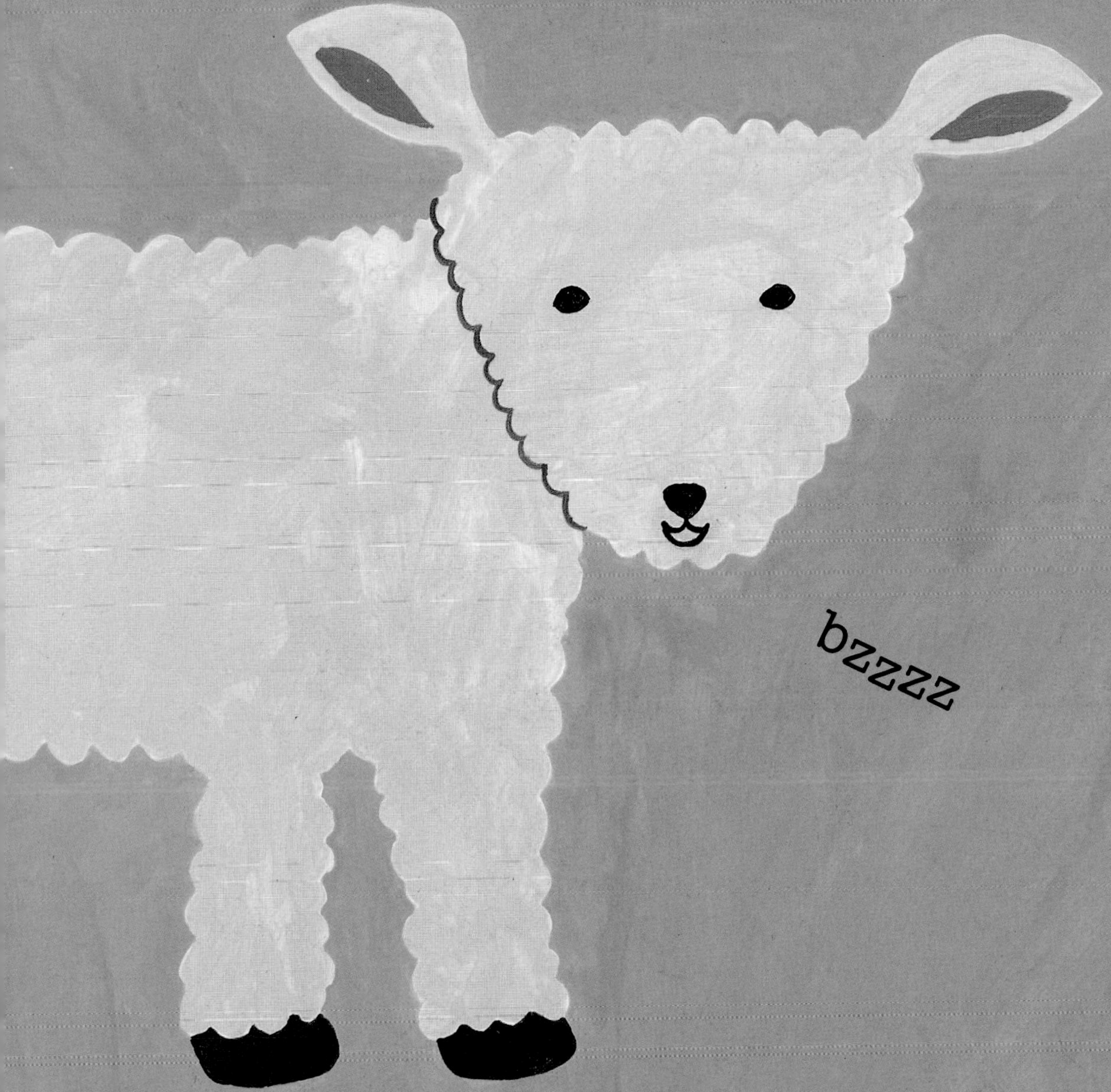

No, bees go buzz.

Do camels cheep?

cheep

cheep

Do butterflies growl?

grrrr

No, but
tigers do!

grrrr

Do rabbits go oink?

oink

oink

oink

oink

oink

No, pigs go oink!

Do owls go hoot in the middle of the night?

Yes they do!
Twit! Twoo!